# What are
# MATERIALS?

First published in 2018 by Wayland
Copyright © Hodder and Stoughton 2018

Wayland
Carmelite House
50 Victoria Embankment
London EC4Y 0DZ
All rights reserved

Managing editor: Victoria Brooker
Creative design: Paul Cherrill

ISBN: 978 1 5263 0662 3

Printed in China

Wayland is a division of
Hachette Children's Books,
an Hachette UK company.
www.hachette.co.uk

# What are

# MATERIALS?

Written by
## KAY BARNHAM

Illustrated by
## MIKE GORDON

WAYLAND

'Hey!' Grandad called, leaning on his spade.
'I've found buried treasure!'
'Yay!' cried Leisha and Poppy.

But when they saw the strange collection of junk, the children were puzzled. Where were the golden necklaces and sparkling jewels? 'This is science treasure,' explained Grandad.

'Can you tell me how all these things
are different to each other?' continued Grandad.

'There's a drinks bottle,

a rusty paint pot

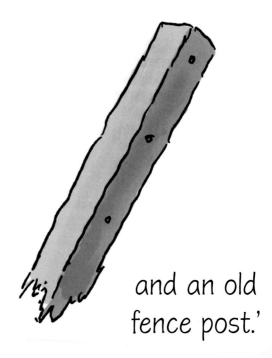

and an old
fence post.'

'Are they all different shapes?' said Leisha.
'They are,' said Grandad, 'but that's not
the answer. Try again!'

Poppy touched each of the objects.
'I know,' she murmured. 'They feel different.
The fence post is knobbly. The bottle is smooth.
And the paint pot is rough. Is that it?'

'You're getting closer.' Grandad grinned.
'They're made from different stuff!' said Leisha.

9

'Yay!' said Poppy.
'Look, the fence post
is wooden, the paint pot is
made from metal and this
bottle is plastic!'

'Spot on!' said Grandad.
'Come on. Let's go and have
some lunch.'

'Each one of these objects was made from
a different material,' explained Grandad.
'Isn't that what curtains are made from?'
asked Leisha.

'Material is another name for cloth,' said Grandad, 'but material is also the word for something used to make things. Wood, plastic and metal are all materials.'

'How many materials are there?' asked Poppy.
'Thousands,' said Grandad. 'Some materials
are natural, which means they come from
plants or animals or the ground.

When humans change natural materials into something else, these are called synthetic materials. For example, sand can be made into glass.'

'Why are there different materials?' asked Leisha.
'Why don't we just make everything
out of the same stuff?
It would be so much easier.'

'Well,' said Grandad, 'why is a fish bowl
made from glass and not wood?'
'That would be silly,' said Poppy, giggling.
'We wouldn't be able to see the fish!'
'Exactly,' said Grandad.

'Glass is transparent,' Grandad went on. 'That means we can see through it. It's also waterproof, so water can't escape. Those are two of the reasons why glass is the perfect material for a fish bowl.'

'I see...' said Leisha thoughtfully. 'So it's
what a material is like that's important?'
Grandad nodded.

'Let me tell you about properties,' said Grandad.
The children looked puzzled.
'That's just a fancy way of saying what a
material is like,' said Grandad, picking up his
newspaper. 'Look, paper is bendy.'

'It's easy to tear too,' said Leisha,
ripping a page in half.
'Hey!' said Grandad. 'That was my crossword!'

'When people make something, they choose the material with the best properties for the job,' said Grandad. 'Imagine you were making a teapot. What properties would the material need to have?'

'It would need to be waterproof,' Poppy said.
'So a wooden teapot would be useless,'
said Leisha added.

'The material needs to be something that can be turned into a special shape,' said Poppy. 'And it needs to stay that shape too. A cake teapot or a jelly teapot would never work!'

'And a teapot can't be made out of newspaper,
wool or cloth either,' said Leisha.
'They would collapse!'

'A teapot must be light enough to lift,' said Poppy. 'Imagine how heavy a rock teapot would be!' Leisha giggled.

'A teapot mustn't melt,' Poppy went on.
'Never use a chocolate teapot,' said Grandad.
'But a china is waterproof and stays the same
shape. It's light and it doesn't melt!' said Leisha.
'China is the perfect material for a teapot!'

'Phew ...' said Grandad.
'All of this thinking has made me hungry.'
'Me too,' said Poppy.
Leisha nodded. 'And me!'

Grandad smiled.
'Then let's eat something that's
been made with these materials – butter,
sugar, flour, eggs, jam and cream.'
'CAKE!' cried the children. 'Yum!'

# NOTES FOR PARENTS AND TEACHERS

The aim of this book is to introduce children to scientific concepts in an entertaining, informative way. Here are some ideas for activities that will encourage them to think further about materials — and have fun doing it!

## ACTIVITIES

1. Look round the house and find five objects.
Then write down which material each of them is made from.
Remember that some objects may be made from more than one thing.

2. Choose one material and then list its properties.

3 Can you rearrange these anagrams to find five phrases to do with materials?

AN ULTRA

EMAIL RAT

PRESTO PIER

ITCHY NETS

FARROW POET

NATURAL, MATERIAL, PROPERTIES, SYNTHETIC, WATERPROOF

## MATERIALS EXPERIMENT

Imagine that you've been asked to build a tower, but you're not allowed to use bricks. Look round the house and see what other materials you can find.

Now use each of these materials to build a tower.

Which was the tallest tower?
Why was that material better than the others?

## DID YOU KNOW ...?

In 1903, the Wright Brothers first flew in an aeroplane made from wood. Now, aeroplanes are made from a metal called aluminium. It is lighter and stronger than wood.

Plastic, oil, paper, cardboard, glass and wood are just some of the different materials that are recycled, so that they can be used again.

Supermarket trolleys, tennis balls and clothes can all be made from plastic!

# BOOKS TO SHARE

**All Kinds of Everything**
*A First Look at Materials*
by Sam Godwin
(Wayland, 2002)

**Everyday Materials**
(Ways into Science)
by Peter Riley
(Watts Publishing, 2016)

**Materials**
(*Amazing Science*)
by Sally Hewitt
(Wayland, 2014)

**Materials**
(*Boom Science* series)
by Georgia Amson-Bradshaw
(Watts Publishing, 2018)

**Materials**
(*Fact Cat* series)
by Izzi Powell
(Wayland, 2018)

**Materials**
(How Does Science Work)
by Carol Ballard
(Wayland, 2014)